UNDERSTANDING GOD'S CALL TO MINISTRY OF WORD & SACRAMENT

IN THE
CUMBERLAND PRESBYTERIAN
CHURCH
GUIDE
FOR INQUIRERS

Pastoral Development Ministry Team

OUR UNITED OUTREACH
Made Possible In Par: By Your Tithe To Our United Outreach

ISBN-13: 978-1475224320
ISBN-10: 147522432X

TABLE OF CONTENTS

The office of Minister of Word and Sacrament *is unique in the life of the church as to responsibility and usefulness. God calls persons and sets them apart for this ministry. The persons who fill this office should be sound in the faith, exemplary in conduct, and competent to perform the duties of the ministry. Persons who become ministers of word and sacrament are due such respect as belongs to their office, but are not by virtue of their office more holy or righteous than other Christians. They share in the same vocation that belongs to all Christians to be witnesses to the gospel in word and deed. They differ from other Christians only with regard to the office to which they are called, which is their station in life.*

The person who fills the office of the ministry has in the scriptures different titles, expressive of various duties:

- *pastor--who has oversight of the people and feeds them with spiritual food and administers the sacraments as signs of God's grace;*

- *minister--who serves Christ in all those ministries to people which belong to the church;*

- *elder or presbyter--who shares in the leadership and government of the church;*

- *evangelist--who bears the glad tidings of salvation through Jesus Christ, appealing to sinners to be reconciled to God;*

- *prophet--who urges people and nations to heed the word of God, warning of the consequences of disobedience;*

- *priest--who intercedes with God through prayer on behalf of others;*

- *preacher--who publicly proclaims the gospel of Christ;*

- *teacher--who explains the scriptures emphasizing the lessons essential to Christian growth.*

These titles do not confer privilege in the church nor designate different grades of office but indicate the scope of responsibilities that belong to the office of ministry.

(Constitution 2.61-2.62)

God Calls,
People Answer

Who? Me? Why would God call me? Why would the God of the universe be aware of me and want me to be a minister?

Perhaps the following common experience will help you to understand how this happens: There is an urgent sense that God is calling us. It never lets up. It is a drawing, a wooing, and a tugging. There may be resistance, reluctance and excuse, and sometimes, refusal. Finally, it becomes a conviction that we are chosen, called and commissioned by God to the ministry.[1]

First, God Calls People to Salvation

The call of God needs to be discussed in the light of our assumption that God calls everyone. It is the belief of the Cumberland Presbyterian Church that God calls all persons into a covenant relationship. It is a call to salvation and an offer of a redemptive relationship with God, a call to a life dedicated to following Jesus Christ. "God acted redemptively in Jesus Christ because of the sins of the world and continues with the same intent in the Holy Spirit to call every person to repentance and faith."[2] "Children of believers are, through the covenant, entitled to the sacrament of baptism and thereby become members of the household of faith. Such children are to receive pastoral oversight, instruction, and the care of the church, with a view that they repent of sin, personally confess Jesus Christ as Lord and Savior, and assume the full responsibilities of church membership."[3] Once we

---

[1] Extracts taken from the book *An Introduction to Christian Ministry For Lay and Clergy Persons in the Cumberland Presbyterian Church* by Morris Pepper.

[2] *Confession of Faith*, Cumberland Presbyterian Church, Section 4.01.

[3] *Constitution*, Cumberland Presbyterian Church, Section 2.13.

have entered into a relationship with God through Jesus Christ, we can expect that there may be other calls to various kinds of service; or to say the least, we have made ourselves open to them.

Then God Calls People to Ministry

We understand the Bible to say that we are not only called to salvation, but to service. Any work we do can be considered as a vocation of God through which we can minister. We believe that God calls lay persons to serve in the church. They serve as elders, deacons, task force members, board members, teachers, administrators, officers in CPWM and similar organizations, leaders of youth and other age groups, and in many other ways. But we also believe that God calls some to be ordained ministers. God will move those people toward ministry in the company of others who are charged with overseeing their growth and supporting their work. Just as God acts to call them personally, God acts through the corporate body of the church to confirm their call. Some will serve as pastors, missionaries, chaplains, seminary professors, pastoral counselors, and in many other areas.

Who Will Answer God's Call?

"Saving faith is response to God, prompted by the Holy Spirit, wherein persons rely solely upon God's grace in Jesus Christ for salvation. Such faith includes trust in the truthfulness of God's promises in the scriptures, sorrow for sin, and determination to serve God and neighbor."[4] You have celebrated the redeeming presence of Christ in your life. Now you feel God's call to ordained ministry in the church and wish to remain open to the leading of the Holy Spirit.

What do you do if you sense a call from God to the Ministry of Word and Sacrament?

---

[4] *Confession of Faith,* Section 4.08.

First, talk with your pastor. If your church does not have a pastor, speak with the moderator of the session who would have been appointed by the presbytery. This person will help you navigate the initial steps in the process. He or she will also be a great resource for you, someone who can relate to the various questions you have and the emotions you undergo. If and when the time comes for you to share your call with the local session, your conversations with the pastor or appointed moderator will allow her or him to support you confidently before the body. The session, when appropriate, will be asked to endorse your coming under care of the presbytery as a candidate for the ministry.

Definition
Of Terms

Approved graduate school of theology: A seminary authorized by a presbytery to provide for the education of that presbytery's ministerial probationers. Courses and credit hours from non-approved seminaries may not be recognized by the presbytery.

Bethel University: The undergraduate/graduate educational institution affiliated with the Cumberland Presbyterian Church and located in McKenzie, Tennessee.

Candidate: A person in the first stage of preparation for the ministry and under the care of a presbytery.

Committee on Clergy Care: A presbytery's agency for the oversight of and support for its clergy members and their families; names may vary with presbyteries.

Committee on Preparation for the Ministry: A presbytery's agency for the oversight of ministerial probationers; names may vary with presbyteries.

Committee on the Ministry: A presbytery's agency for the oversight of ministerial probationers and ordained clergy, unless these responsibilities are divided between two committees.

Confession of Faith **(1984):** The creedal statement and governmental standards for the Cumberland Presbyterian Church and Cumberland Presbyterian Church in America. Major divisions are:

Confession of Faith	Constitution
Rules of Discipline	Directory for Worship
Rules of Order	

Constitution: The document, contained in the *Confession of Faith*, delineating the government of the Cumberland Presbyterian Church and Cumberland Presbyterian Church in America.

Licentiate: The status of a ministerial probationer between candidate and ordained; licentiates are authorized to preach under the supervision of the presbytery.

Memphis Theological Seminary (MTS): A graduate school of theology affiliated with the Cumberland Presbyterian Church and located in Memphis, Tennessee.

Minister of Word and Sacrament: A person who has been ordained into the ministry of the Cumberland Presbyterian Church or Cumberland Presbyterian Church in America.

Ordinand: A person who has been recommended for ordination as a Minister of Word and Sacrament but has not been ordained yet.

Ordination: The act of a presbytery to set a person a part for the ministry of Word and Sacrament.

Particular church: As used in the *Constitution*, a congregation of the Cumberland Presbyterian Church or Cumberland Presbyterian Church in America.

Pastor: The title for an ordained minister who has been installed by the presbytery to provide spiritual leadership in a particular congregation. **ALSO Associate/ Assistant Pastor:** The title for an ordained minister who has been installed by the presbytery to assist the pastor in providing spiritual leadership in a particular congregation.

Presbytery: The primary governing body within the Cumberland Presbyterian Church or Cumberland Presbyterian Church in America and consisting of ordained ministers and elders elected to represent sessions within a defined area.

Probationer: A person preparing for the ministry under the care of a presbytery. Probationers may be candidates or licentiates.

Program of Alternate Studies (PAS): A Cumberland Presbyterian Church program for the education of ministerial probationers who, in the opinion of their presbyteries, cannot reasonably attend seminary.

Provisional Status: An ethnic-ordained minister desiring to come into the Cumberland Presbyterian Church from another denomination, serving in a cross-cultural ministry, and whose educational preparation does not yet meet CPC standards, may be received under Provisional Status with all rights and privileges of ordination.

Reformed/Presbyterian tradition: Refers to those churches that trace their roots to John Calvin, a key player in the Protestant Reformation. Theologically, these churches emphasize the sovereignty of God, the authority of scripture and salvation by grace through faith. They follow a representative form of government led by elders or "presbyters."

Rules of Discipline: The section of the *Confession of Faith* setting forth procedures for dealing with misconduct or unusual situations within the church.

Session: The governing body of a particular church (congregation), consisting of the pastor and members elected by the congregation.

Stated Supply: An ordained minister, a licentiate, or a candidate approved by the presbytery to serve as minister of a particular church (congregation). A stated supply is not an installed pastor and may perform only those pastoral functions set forth in the *Constitution*.

"Under care": The description of the status of a ministerial probationer under the supervision of a presbytery.

How The Church
Is Governed

"The purpose of church government is to aid the church in performing its mission."[5]

The easiest way to understand Presbyterian church government is to think back to what you learned in high school civics. (In fact, our judicial system is patterned after Presbyterian church law, also called polity.) In our national judicial system:

- A federal magistrate acts at the directives of higher courts in handling less serious matters, thus allowing the superior courts to focus upon the more serious matters
- More serious civil or criminal matters are heard in district court, which renders verdicts in these cases
- The court of appeals rules on the regularity of procedure and/or conformity to law in the decisions of district courts
- The Supreme Court rules on the adherence to the Constitution in the decisions of the lower courts

In a general way, the courts — commonly called "judicatories" — in the Presbyterian system of government parallel our federal court system. Those judicatories are

- The **session** of a congregation (called a particular church in the *Constitution*). It consists of the pastor and members elected by the congregation. (For a list of sessional responsibilities, see the *Constitution* 4.5.)

- The **presbytery** consisting of the ordained ministers and elders elected by sessions to represent congregations within a specific area. Presbyteries have oversight of congregations, ministers and probationers within its bounds

---

[5] Preamble to the Constitution, *Confession of Faith*, 1984

and hear appeals brought from sessions. (For a list of presbyterial responsibilities, see the *Constitution* 5.6.)

- The **synod** consists of at least three presbyteries within a prescribed area. Synods have oversight of presbyteries and hear appeals brought from them. Some also have program responsibilities. (For a list of synodic responsibilities, see the *Constitution* 8.5.)

- The **General Assembly**, the highest judicatory in the church, has oversight of the entire church, including doctrine, polity, discipline, property and judicatories. It also hears appeals. (For a list of General Assembly responsibilities, see the *Constitution* 9.4.)

A set of checks and balances comes into play at each level of church government:

- Sessions elect delegates to presbytery
- Presbyteries have oversight of ministers, probationers and sessions within their bounds; they also hear appeals from sessions
- Synods have oversight of presbyteries and hear appeals from presbyteries
- Delegates to synods are elected by presbyteries
- The General Assembly has oversight responsibilities for the entire church
- Presbyteries elect commissioners to General Assembly and must approve changes in the *Confession of Faith*, *Constitution* and *Catechism* referred to them by the General Assembly.

Each judicatory serves a unique function and has a specific oversight responsibility. However, the presbytery is the pivotal church court. In its oversight of congregations and ordained ministers, it functions as a bishop. Presbyteries also hold another important balance of power or responsibility. They elect minister and elder commissioners to meetings of the General Assembly.

Because presbyteries, meeting at stated intervals, do not have the time or expertise to conduct programs and exercise oversight, they assign these responsibilities to *ad hoc* or standing committees and/or commissions (See the *Constitution* 3.10.) These agencies focus upon their assigned spheres of ministry and make recommendations to their presbyteries.

Oversight of ministerial probationers (candidates, licentiates, ordinands) and ordained clergy may be given by a presbytery to its Committee on the Ministry. Or these responsibilities may be divided between a Committee on Preparation for the Ministry (or similar function/name) and a Committee on Clergy Care (or similar function/name). Regardless of where a presbytery lodges these responsibilities, "oversight" involves both supervision and support.

Stresses upon the ordained clergy and their families can be both sharp and acute. It is, therefore, important that members of presbyteries' committees charged with oversight of ordained clergy be aware of these stressors. They should also convey a spirit of understanding and support where needed and impartial discipline where appropriate.

Oversight of clergy probationers also requires sensitive, mature judgment and approachability. Probation is a time of exploring the nature of God's call as well as preparing for ministry. Committee members must always remember that their presbyteries ordain not just for their presbytery but also for the entire church. It is important, therefore, that the ordination standards contained in the *Constitution* (6.34) be honored.

PART ONE
Overview Of The Process
For Ordination

1. Why Ordain A Person To Be
A Minister Of Word And Sacrament?

In the Cumberland Presbyterian Church a person is ordained as a Minister of Word and Sacrament. We, as a church body, do not specifically ordain people as pastor, missionary, Christian educator, etc.

We believe that ministry can take many forms because people have been blessed with gifts from God that are very unique and special. We recognize that people are called to different ministries. Also we recognize that a person's call from God may evolve and change over time. That is why we do not specifically ordain people to a specific ministry area. We need to respect God's freedom to work in people's lives, maturing, expanding and growing their call to ministry.

We feel, as a church, that the educational requirements for a Minister of Word and Sacrament are sufficient to prepare and sustain a minister for any type of ministry that God might call that person to. If we ordained people to a certain ministry, for example Christian education, the educational requirements for that track of ministry would need to be specific to that call. But the problem arises if that person is later called to, for example, serve as a missionary. It might then be necessary to go back to school to fulfill the requirements for ordination as a missionary.

We intentionally leave this category broad so that God can lead, guide and work in our ministers for the purposes that God intends.

"While the type of ministry most basic to the life of the church is that of a pastor, God has given different gifts to ministers of the word and sacrament and the church recognizes various types of ministry. Presbytery may authorize ministers to exercise their gifts not only as pastors of particular churches but as teachers of religion in various kinds of schools, editors of religious publications, chaplains to the military forces and to various types of institutions, missionaries, evangelists, counselors, administrators of church programs and institutions, directors of Christian education in particular churches, and as leaders in other fields of service directly related to the church."

(*Constitution*, 2.64)

2. So You're Sensing A Call: Mapping The Journey To Ordination In The Cumberland Presbyterian Church

If you're reading this, you're probably thinking about becoming a candidate for ministry. Presbyterial Committees on the Ministry/Preparation will be familiar with this material, also. But this information is directed primarily toward you, the potential candidate. It aims to describe in some detail the process for responding to God's call in the Cumberland Presbyterian Church.

The Cumberland Presbyterian Church believes in an internal call. God moves on the hearts of persons, drawing them toward ordained ministry. Yet, this internal call needs the external confirmation of the church. As you move toward ordination, you will do so in the company of others who are charged with overseeing your growth. These people will help you discern if ordination is in fact your vocation in life. Just as God acts to call you personally, God acts through the corporate body of the church to support your work and confirm your call.

So, what do you do when you sense God may be calling you to ordained ministry?

First, talk with your pastor.

Your pastor will help you navigate the initial steps in the process. He or she also can relate to the various questions you have and the emotions you are feeling. When the time comes for you to share your call with the local session, your conversations with the pastor will allow her or him to support you confidently before the body. If your church does not have a pastor, you should speak with the minister appointed by the presbytery to moderate your session. One of the elders can help you know who this person is.

After informal conversations with the pastor, you will meet with the session. It's the first official step in becoming a candidate for ministry.

The session has the responsibility to endorse you as a candidate. You must be a member in good standing of a Cumberland Presbyterian congregation, and you must have the session's endorsement before the presbytery accepts you as a candidate. Your family knows you best. A recommendation from the leadership of your church family speaks volumes. The local session clerk will write a letter to the presbytery's Committee on the Ministry/Preparation in your support, provided the session votes to recommend you. (*Constitution* 6.12)

The presbyterial Committee on the Ministry/Preparation will want to meet with you after they receive the session's letter.

Each committee handles its interviews in its own way. But certainly the members will want to hear your experience of the call. Your work with your pastor and session should prepare you well for this meeting. Be honest with the committee. Share with them your fears as well as your joys as you consider your call. The more they know you, the better they can help you. The more real you are, the more they will want to help you.

The committee has the responsibility to recommend you as a CANDIDATE at the next meeting of presbytery.

You will attend this meeting. Presbytery has the responsibility of examining you. So, persons may ask questions of you from the floor. You may be asked to share your sense of call. Then, in keeping with the *Constitution* of the church, the following questions will be put to you.

I.   *As far as you know your heart, do you believe yourself to be called by God to the office of the Christian ministry?*

II. *Do you promise, in reliance upon the grace of God, to maintain a Christian character and conduct, and to be diligent and faithful in making full preparation for the ministry?*

III. *Do you promise to work with the presbytery through its committee on the ministry in matters that pertain to your preparation for the ministry?*

IV. *Do you now desire to be received by this presbytery as a candidate for the ministry in the Cumberland Presbyterian Church/Cumberland Presbyterian Church in America?*

If you answer these questions affirmatively, and the presbytery so votes, you will be received as a candidate under care of the presbytery. You will attend all subsequent meetings of presbytery after your acceptance.

Presbytery will care for you through the Committee on the Ministry or its equivalent. You will meet with them at least once a year. The committee probably will appoint one member to serve as your liaison or mentor. This person will stay in close contact with you as you move through the requirements of ordination. But you should always feel free to contact the committee when you need help. These persons are charged to support you and to struggle with you. The committee also may provide financial support for your education. The amount and type of support vary from presbytery to presbytery.

Some seminaries provide excellent financial help to seminary students. For example, our denominational seminary, Memphis Theological Seminary, provides service loans for probationers pursuing their divinity degree.

Ordained ministry (what we often call the Ministry of Word and Sacrament or the Gospel ministry, and what we most typically associate with the pastorate) requires a four-year degree from a college or university. Exceptions are sometimes made for those whose circumstances make such an education highly impractical. In these cases, only with presbytery approval, candidates may enter the Program of Alternate Studies. The candidate enrolled in PAS is required to complete a list of college courses totaling 60 hours. With the plethora of community colleges now available, those courses are very much within reach.

Preparation for ministry includes more than formal education. Committees oversee the development of the whole person toward ministry. So it is within their purview to explore a candidate's spiritual life, emotional health and giftedness. Candidates may be asked to submit to psychological examination from a trained professional. They may also be asked to complete spiritual gifts inventories. Such instruments shall not be used to decide if a person is called or not, but will serve to increase a candidate's knowledge of self (strengths as well as weaknesses) and to help identify goals for growth.

As you are moving through candidacy, the committee will continue to help you clarify your call. They will ask regularly if you feel led toward ordained ministry.

Once the committee is satisfied with your growth and development, you will be recommended for LICENSURE by the committee.

The presbytery will examine you on the floor prior to licensure.

Does being licensed mean you are given responsibilities you did not have as a candidate? No, but licensure is a sign that you are making progress and that the church recognizes your growth. It's a significant mile marker toward the full embrace of your calling. The questions asked to licentiates are listed below:

I.   *Do you believe the scriptures of the Old and New Testaments to be the inspired word of God, the authority for faith and practice?*

II. *Do you sincerely receive and adopt the Confession of Faith of the Cumberland Presbyterian Church/Cumberland Presbyterian Church in America as containing the essential doctrines taught in the Holy Scriptures?*

III. *Do you promise to promote the peace, unity, and purity of the church?*

IV. *Do you promise continued cooperation with the presbytery through its committee on the ministry as you continue preparation for ordination, and as you perform those functions of ministry which pertain to a licentiate, as set forth in the Constitution?*

Those licensed are required to complete a Master of Divinity degree from an accredited seminary before ordination. If you have been accepted in the PAS program, you must complete a three-year course of study for ordination. The PAS program administers these courses through its director.

Once educational requirements are complete and the committee is satisfied with your progress, you will be eligible for ORDINATION.

To be ordained, you must receive a formal call to ministry from a congregation, hospital, hospice program, university, etc., and must sustain examination by presbytery.

If you answer affirmatively and presbytery so votes, a time and date will be set for your ordination. At the service for ordination, you will be asked the following questions:

I. *Do you believe the scriptures of the Old and New Testaments to be the inspired word of God, the authority for faith and practice?*

II. *Do you sincerely receive and adopt the Confession of Faith of the Cumberland Presbyterian Church/Cumberland Presbyterian Church in America as containing the essential doctrines taught in the Holy Scriptures?*

III. *Do you approve of and promise to uphold the government of the Cumberland Presbyterian Church/Cumberland Presbyterian Church in America?*

IV. *In participating as a minister in the judicatories of the church, do you promise to share in a responsible way in the decisions that are made, to abide by those decisions, and to promote the welfare of the church?*

V. *As far as you know your heart, have you been induced by the Holy Spirit to answer the call to the ministry from love of God and neighbor and a sincere desire to glorify God and advance his Kingdom in the world?*

VI.   As God may enable you, do you promise to be zealous and faithful
      in maintaining the truths of the gospel and the purity and peace
      of the church, irrespective of any opposition that may arise to you
      on that account?

VII. Do you promise to be faithful and diligent in the exercise of all
      your duties as a Christian and a minister of the gospel, and
      endeavor to so conduct yourself both privately and publicly as not
      to give offense to Christ and his church?

Once you have answered the questions affirmatively, you will kneel. Ministers of the presbytery will lay hands on you as a prayer is offered. When you rise and the declaration is made, you will be an ordained minister with all the responsibility and respect that accompany that title.

Sometimes, a person becomes a candidate, even a licentiate, only to discover that he or she is not called to ordained ministry. If you are faced with this difficult situation, you should keep these things in mind. Most ministers struggle to understand their calling. In this you are not alone. Neither is there any shame in removing yourself from the committee's care. It would be much worse to save embarrassment by continuing in a vocation to which God has not called you. Being honest and open with the committee as you work through the process will lay a good foundation should you need to change courses before ordination.

Consult the *Constitution* of the Cumberland Presbyterian Church, section 6.00, for a more formal description of the above process. The *Constitution* can be found online at www.cumberland.org.

PART TWO
God's Call To Ministry

3. Biblical Basis Of Call
Presented At The Christian Education Conference
November 1981 By John Ed Gardner

Obviously, I am here, and you are here; but how did it happen that we in particular got to this place on this occasion? We came from many localities and we represent a number of professions, trades, and careers. Some of us think of ourselves as ordained clergy, but others identify themselves as lay persons. But I suppose that diversity is not really important in this instance for we are all here for a common purpose. Across whatever vocational and, or ecclesiastical differences that separate us in a common tie that unites us in a common cause and common purpose.

I suspect we all got to this place and occasion in basically the same fashion. We might describe the specifics a bit differently, but in the final analysis we were invited, enlisted, urged, and otherwise prevailed upon to attend this meeting. We were "called" to be here. There is a common element running through this diversity of the call; in every instance the church was instrument of the call. In some instances it was the General Assembly Board; in other instances the church is identified as the presbytery or synod or one of their agencies. The local church has spoken as well to many of you.

Now, I would like to examine some of these affirmations in the light of certain Biblical precepts.

It is God who calls! Let me affirm that it is God who takes the initiative in the encounter we have with him. I prefer to think of the engagement with God as "encounter" which is dialogical in nature, rather than as "confrontation" in which God alone acts to call us to commitment.

Having said that it is God who calls, I must immediately confess that how he does so is not so easily declared; his ways of doing so are many and far less precise in description. I think it may become quite apparent as we pursue our subject for the evening that the manner and nature of the experience of being called is quite personal. Indeed, each person is entitled to her/his own description and interpretation of the experience. No norms for the experience can be projected except to say that we understand God to be the prime mover in the experience, granted he may make his will known to us through many and diverse avenues or instruments of his grace. However it happens, the individual is likely to interpret the experience in the light of her/his own personal input. There can be no uniformity in that regard; however, as we explore the nature of the experience, we may find some common ground for understanding.

We are a community of called people; called to a community of faith, to be God's chosen people; a special people to fulfill a particular mission in the world. This calling is extended to everyone though some do not hear and respond to the invitation. In the ultimate sense, the calling is to salvation. Paul speaks of this call when in addressing the Romans (Romans 1:6-7) he declares, "You who have heard the call and belong to Jesus Christ. I send greetings to all of you in Rome whom God loves and has called to be his dedicated people." With the same understanding he addresses the Church of Corinth (I Corinthians 1:24) "to those who have heard his call, Jews and Greeks alike, he is the power of God and the wisdom of God."

From the same perspective of Jude (Jude 1) speaks of the called when he writes, "From Jude, servant of Jesus Christ and brother of James, to those whom God has called, who live in the love of God the Father and in the safekeeping of Jesus Christ."

The writer of Revelation (Rev. 17:14) has the same understanding of what it means to be called to salvation when he declares that the Lamb who is "Lord of Lords and King of Kings" will triumph "and his victory will be shared by his followers, called and chosen and faithful."

When Paul wrote to Timothy (II Timothy 1:9) he witnessed to the calling which is extended in the hope of winning a faith response. He says, "It is he who brought us salvation and called us to a dedicated life, not for any merit of ours but of his own purpose and his own grace." "Called" with the intent of "dedication" is crucial to our understanding of our role and status as follower of Jesus Christ.

All calling of whatever nature seems predicated upon the call to salvation, the intended consequence of which is one's inclusion and participation in the community of faith. Any other or subsequent call is secondary to this. Indeed, one may assume or expect that persons, having heard the call to salvation and having responded affirmatively, have made themselves susceptible to a call to particular services, ministries and, or vocations.

Certainly there are, and always have been, those who understood themselves to be called to vocation. Insofar as such vocations are understood to differ from the call to service incumbent upon every follower, they differ in their structural character as pertains to the manner and function of the institution. The mission which they represent is held in common by all the people of faith.

Call to Vocation

Let us take a look at the call identified with vocation. In the Old Testament we readily observe that calling was at times construed to imply a particular vocation. Moses was called through a burning bush to lead the people Israel; Samuel, as a lad, heard a voice in Eli's temple; Aaron understood himself to be called to serve as priest; David was called from his role as a shepherd boy to be a king; and Jeremiah understood himself appointed a prophet while in his mother's womb.

In the New Testament Jesus sometimes called persons to follow him and vocation was implied. Examples are in Mark 1:20 where it is reported that Jesus saw James and John, sons of Zebedee, overhauling their fishing nets and "He called them; and leaving their father Zebedee in the boat with the hired men, they went off to follow him." In like fashion Mark 3:13 reports that "He went up into the hill country and called the men he wanted; and they went and joined him." The account goes on to say, "He appointed twelve as his companion, whom he would send out to proclaim the Gospel, with commission to drive out devils." In an altogether different kind of experience but one nonetheless direct, Saul of Tarsus was awakened to the awesome demands of the Gospel while on the road to Damascus.

Call to Office

To be "called" sometimes refers to a particular office. Paul understood himself to have such a call (Romans 1:1). "From Pau servant of Christ Jesus, Apostle by God's call, set apart for service of the Gospel." Likewise, from I Corinthians 1:1, we read, "From Paul, Apostle of Jesus Christ at God's Call and by God's will."

In the letter to the Hebrews (Hebrews 5:4) the writer shares the same view of certain experiences of being called to priesthood when he affirms, "And nobody arrogates the honor to himself: he is called by God, as indeed Aaron was."

Luke, in his record of the Acts of the Apostles, reports on how certain persons were called to particular office; witness, "Set Barnabas and Saul apart for me, to do the work to which I have called them." He reports well on Paul's response to his vision to come over to Macedonia, "after he had seen this vision we at once set about getting a passage to Macedonia. Concluding that God had called us to bring them the good news." (Acts 16:10).

Call to Mission

However one may understand her/his personal experience, and however that experience may be identified, all calling merges at the point of our common mission as the people of God. The church is called to a singular mission. The church is one body with Christ as its one head. This singularity is evidenced by history as well as theology. The church as a covenant community affirms a continuity that spans the full scope of Judeo-Christian tradition. What belongs to and is the prerogative of its individual constituents is, also, the heritage of the collective body. The oneness of the church is witnessed by the parity of its membership; there are no orders, rank, hierarchy in the church. The distinction between clergy and laity is functional and official only. Both share in the one mission of the church, distinctions in vocation notwithstanding.

"You are a chosen race, the King's priests, the holy nation, God's own people, chosen to proclaim the wonderful acts of God, who called you out of darkness into his marvelous light" (I Peter 2:0. Royalty and priesthood in Jewish history had always been understood, though vested in individuals, to bear the responsibility of ministering to the whole people. Now Christians were to understand to understand themselves as a chosen people, called out, to proclaim the wonderful works of God. This calling came not to certain of them but to the whole people, a chosen race, called even as God had chosen individuals in former times. The task of this chosen race, the people of God, found its fulfillment in the new community of Christians, a holy nation. They held in common one mission. The Apostle Paul appropriately observed, "though we are many, we are one body in union with Christ, and we are all joined to each other as different parts of one body: (Romans 12:5).

The New Testament knows but one vocation, and that is common to all followers of Christ. All are called to become children of God and to live in the world as such. This living means that we must manifest a Christian presence wherever we are and under whatever circumstances we are to live. We are called to a common discipleship, to repentance and the affirmation of a common faith.

This mission finds expression in a common fellowship where participants are not identified as the "good guys with the white hats;" but rather as repentant sinners who are distinguished by their awareness that they are loved and redeemed by God through

Christ. We know ourselves not so much as a lovely people but as a loved people. Identity is gained only through repentance and faith as we are reconciled to God through faith in Jesus Christ. Our life together is made possible not by sharing the same background, culture, race, or status, but by sharing a new life, a common calling, mission, and destiny in Christ. To share that calling falls indiscriminately upon all who know themselves to be a part of the community of faith.

Among us prevails a diversity of gifts. There is a wide range of gifts of service and devotion possessed by men and women of every walk and station in life. "And his gifts were that some should be apostles, some prophets, some evangelists, some pastors and teachers, for the equipment of the saints, for the work of ministry for building up the body of Christy" (Ephesians 4:11-12). Such a diversity cannot be construed as the exclusive domain of the clergy. We affirm the doctrine of the common priesthood of all believers; by which we do not mean that we simply do not need a confessor, rather, we affirm the commonality of our responsibility and mission to and for each other and the world. No fact of human concern and caring falls outside the realm of that priesthood. That is not to question or minimize the position that there is an area of responsibility and ministry which the church has appropriately delegated or assigned to appropriate one's of its constituency who may be ordained, set apart, to work in particular leadership roles for the total group. However, they do not on that account enter upon a separate or different ministry and mission.

Our common mission further embraces the call to be an instrument of God's grace. The laity are, I think, uniquely equipped for this ministry. Such a mission aspires through the life of the church to unite persons in a new humanity which God offers through fellowship in the life of Christ. The church is not really important as an end in itself, but only as it becomes a means through which we fulfill our calling as instruments of his grace.

The mission we share is also expressed through proclamation oftentimes narrowly construed as the work of preaching. That is too restrictive a view of proclamation. D. T. Niles, long ago, in his book

Preacher's Task and Stone of Stumbling, pointed to the enlistment, calling, of the whole church to be an army proclaiming the Kingdom of Christ. At the very center of this task are the varied ministries of educating, nurturing and equipping people for the missions of being the people of God in the world and enabling them to enter upon the venture of witnessing and ministering in Christ's name wherever they may be gathered or dispersed.

The church, understood as the people of God, is both the agent and the authenticating voice of the call. The call has always required the legitimization of the church, whether the call be defined in terms of clergy or lay roles. Such a contention does not bring into question either the nature or intensity of the experience through which one believes the call to have come; rather, it is an affirmation of the role which the church historically and theologically continues to occupy in God's order of ministry in the world.

Both clergy and laity share in this ministry of calling in extending and in receiving the call; granted separateness in office, but no division in ministry. Near the end of the first century and into the second, the church lost the emphasis upon the priesthood of believers and drew attention to the separation of laity and clergy, thus formalizing a particular office for clergy. Such a separation has continued. While the Reformation called attention to the doctrine; it did not significantly diminish the distortion.

I think it is most appropriate that we are continuing to address the issue, especially as it pertains to the church's understanding of the Biblical injunction of call. It is urgent that the church recover her role and voice in issuing the call. There can be no effective calling apart from the church. Though all of us may understand our experience of being called in personal terms, the validity of what we have experienced is of necessity subjected to the scrutiny and judgment of the church. It cannot be otherwise; the only alternative is a totally inadequate and unacceptable individualism.

We may be instructed regarding the role of the people of God in the call by remembering how the eleven acted to call Mathias to so exalted a pace as apostleship (Acts 1:26). When the Lord was no longer bodily present with them, they very responsibly became the body to call and install one to replace Judas.

In as awesome an event as Paul experienced on the Road to Damascus, God chose to use those of the church to authenticate the call. God surely chose Paul to be his instrument to bring his name before the nations; yet to bring to fruition that call, God engaged Ananias of Damascus, a disciple, to be a means of grace in bringing Paul to an understanding and acceptance of the ministry to which God was leading (Acts 22:14-15). It was Ananias who informed Paul that God had appointed him a witness to the world.

On another and later occasion the Apostles and elders, with the consent and agreement of the whole church when confronted with the problem of Judiazers in the church at Antioch, sent Judas and Silas along with Paul and Barnabas to help allay the strife.

The church as God's agent of call has not restricted or limited her voice to those who are to be clergypersons. It has only restricted ordination as it relates to authenticating persons for ministry of the word and sacrament. That limitation I support but with no assumption that any distinction in "calling" is implied. It seems to me that the Biblical witness to call does not so warrant. However, there is a sense in which the word and sacraments are instructed to the church, not to any of us as individuals, and it is appropriate for the church to devise and honor such practices as it feels appropriate to assume its responsible stewardship of that trust. It is in this sense that ordination witnesses to the church's act of setting apart for a particular office and function those who are otherwise called to the ministry of the whole church. In ordination, then, we are not talking about called persons versus uncalled ones; we are talking rather of how the church collectively exercises a major responsibility.

The church that acts dynamically and irrevocable in authenticating call for this special area of her ministry certainly may act with equal and unrivaled authority in calling persons to engage in the many and varied ministries of her corporate life. When the church calls, it calls as the voice and instrument of God's grace. When the church call for laity as well as clergy, her voice is equally authentic and should be equally compelling in the responses which any of her constituents may make.

Conclusion

I can now summarize certain conclusions with regard to calling which I wish to put in some order.

First, "calling" relates quite broadly to the manner and purpose of our encounter with God in his call and offer of salvation to every person. God calls each and all of us to redemption and to a dedicated life. This is without respect to vocation or station in life.

Second, the experience of being "called" relates, as well, to the person's understanding of how she/he is to live out her/his witness and ministry in the world. In this sense "calling" has to do with how the individual understands God to intervene in her/his life. In this context the content and structure of call is purely personal and the character of the experience seems more determined by the character of the individual than by any peculiarity of the divine initiative toward one person as distinguished from another.

Third, "calling" may, and does, take on additional meaning for those who are especially sensitive to needs in the church and the world and who are disposed to be responsive to those needs. Such calling may embrace special vocation, particular ministries, or dedication to a particular cause or need. However, such a sense of calling may just as appropriately be experienced by someone who fulfills the calling in the context of a so-called secular vocation.

Fourth, the variance in the call experienced by laity and clergy is primarily a difference in intensity and interpretation of the experience occasioned by the extent to which such a calling is disruptive of what would otherwise be normal occupational behavior.

Fifth, the church as the people of God may, but does not necessarily, initiate the experience of call for particular persons. However, the church is never less than the indirect agent of call creating both the condition and awareness which enable persons to confront the needs for which the call to a ministry is occasioned. It is not inappropriate that the church directly voice the call to as many as are disposed to hear.

Sixth, however experienced, and however understood, it is the church which validates the call whether to lay ministry or to a clergy role. Even though one may profess an individualized and personal experience, the same cannot be assumed as valid without the corroborating judgment of the church. This is equally apparent in calls to roles as clergy and as lay persons. That which legitimates a person's "call" is the authenticating voice of the church.

Finally, whether or not the church has adequate leadership for her mission in the world depends finally upon our understanding and honoring of the voice and role of the church in "calling." It is incumbent upon the church that its voice be clear and its call firm and confident.

4. "The Call" In Historical And Theological Perspective

A study paper prepared for the Permanent Committee on Theology and Social Concerns by Jay Earheart-Brown

The Call of God

The 1984 *Confession of Faith of the* Cumberland Presbyterian Churches begins with the affirmation that "God speaks to the human family."[6] In various ways, through many different means, we confess that "by word and action God invites persons into a covenant relationship."[7] This invitation of God, is the foundation of any Christian understanding of the call. The Christian life is a life lived in response to the call of God. Thus Paul refers to Christians as those who are "called to be saints" (Rom. 1:7, 1 Cor. 1:2). The Greek word for church, while commonly used in the Greek world for any assembly, is literally, "those who are called out" (*ekklesia*). God takes the initiative to call together, to assemble a people and fashion them for God's purpose in the world.

The history of Israel as God's chosen people was grounded in God's call to Abraham and Sarah to leave their homeland to follow God's directing. God's intent for the people was further intensified in God's calling of the descendants of Abraham and Sarah out of Egypt in the Exodus. Israel is chosen, called, elected by God not because of the people's righteousness, our power, or any other intrinsic quality. The nation is called not to special privilege, but to be a "light to the nations." God's call to Israel, then, is a part of God's larger intention to reclaim all God's wayward children.

---

[6] Heading for section 1.00, *Confession of Faith*, in the *Confession of Faith and Government of the Cumberland Presbyterian Church and the Second Cumberland Presbyterian Church* (Memphis: Frontier Press, 1984), p. 1. Hereafter *COF*.
[7] *COF*, sec. 1.03, p. 1.

Jesus' public ministry began with his calling of the twelve. They followed Jesus, according to the Gospel accounts, not from their own initiative, but in response to Jesus' call to leave their nets (and other occupations) and follow him. In Jesus' death and resurrection, those disciples became convinced that God was calling all people, the Jews and gentiles alike, into covenant relationship. The preaching and teaching of the earliest Christians was the means by which the call of God went out from Jerusalem into the Greco-Roman world and beyond.

God's call to all people to salvation and life, what the *Confession* refers to, as "the call to covenant relationship," is the foundation of any adequate theology of the call. This primary call of God is what the early Puritan theologians referred to as the "general calling." It is a calling that all who respond to God in faith hear. It is common to all Christians. The *Confession* also refers to it as "the call and work of the Holy Spirit:"

> The call and work of the Holy Spirit is solely of God's grace and is not a response to human merit. The call precedes all desire, purpose, and intention of the sinner to come to Christ. While it is possible for all to be saved with it, none can be saved without it. Whoever will, therefore, may be saved, but not apart from the illuminating influence of the Holy Spirit. (*1984 COF*, section 4.03)

All Christians are called to salvation; all Christians are called to the ministry of Jesus Christ.

The general call of God is also a call to the church, the people of God, the community of faith. It is more than an individual call; it is fully corporate as well. The church's task is to ask not only what God is calling each of us to do, but also what God is calling the church to be and do. As the *Confession* says, "The church is called into being and exists to reach out to those who have not experienced God's grace in Christ, and to nourish them with all the means of grace" (*1984 COF*, section 5.29).

The Call and Christian Ethics

This invitation, this call, while fundamentally a call to covenant relationship with God, is at the same time all call to a particular way of life. Like God's call to Israel, it is not a call to special favor. It is a call to righteousness, love and service. The ethical dimensions of God's call are raised through considering the question, "What does it mean, in practical terms, to live in covenant relationship with God?" Paul's ethical instructions to the early churches can be summarized in the counsel to "lead a life worthy of the calling to which you have been called" (Eph. 4:1). God's call is a call to a specific way of life patterned after the life and ministry of Jesus. The ethical dimensions of God's call flow from God's grace in Jesus Christ, and are incumbent on all who would live as God's people in the world.

The task of Christian ethics is to specify what it means to live in response to God's call. This task is often difficult. While the general contours of a life lived in covenant relationship with God are clear from reading the Scriptures, Christians often disagree on how those contours inform specific decisions in specific circumstances. How should Christians respond to situations the Biblical writers could not have foreseen? Christians in good conscience may disagree on how God's general calling to the life of faith may best be demonstrated in specific situations. But they cannot escape the imperative to live out the call to discipleship in every sphere of their lives.

A second type of difficulty arises through competing claims on one's attention and energy. How does one manage the competing callings to be a faithful and loving husband or wife, son or daughter, father or mother, with the calling to be a responsible employee or employer, and the calling to responsible membership in the community of faith? Sometimes the deepest ethical conflicts arise over how we are to relate the overlapping callings and commitments that make up our lives.

The call to covenant relationship with God, then, is at the same time a call to covenant relationship with the people of God, in service to the world. It is not a call to privilege or status; it is not a call to individual salvation apart from the community of faith and the life of sacrificial service. The one call of God in Jesus Christ is a call to love God with our heart and soul and strength and our neighbors as ourselves.

Particular Callings and the Idea of Vocation

Historically, the people of God have also interpreted the call of God to encompass callings to particular ministries both within and outside the covenant community, and to specific tasks in specific circumstances. Such particular calls are given to individuals within the community of faith, but are at the same time intended to serve the one call of God to faith and service. One aspect of the particular calling of God for individuals relates to how one earns a living.

Before the toleration of Christianity in the Roman Empire, those who responded to God's calling to the life of faith in Jesus Christ and participation in the covenant community were liable to suffer serious consequences. Those consequences included disruption of family relationships, alienation from the Roman government (including imprisonment and even death), and, for some at least, a change in occupation. *The Apostolic Tradition* of *Hippolytus*, written around 215 A.D., gives instruction to the churches about those who seek membership:

> Inquiry shall be made about the crafts and professions of those who are brought for instruction. If a man is a brothel-keeper, let him cease or be rejected. If anyone is a sculptor or a painter, let them be instructed not to make idols; let them cease or be rejected. If anyone is an actor or gives theatrical performances, let him cease or be rejected. He who teaches children had best cease, but if he has no craft, let him have permission. Similarly, a charioteer who competes in the games, or goes to them, let him cease or be rejected. One who is a gladiator or teaches gladiators to fight, or one who fights with beasts in the games, or a public official employed on gladiatorial business, let him cease or be rejected. If anyone is a priest, or keeper of idols, let him cease or be rejected. A soldier under authority shall not kill a man. If he is ordered

to, he shall not carry out the order; nor shall he take the oath. If he is unwilling, let him be rejected. He who has the power of the sword, or is a magistrate of a city who wears the purple, let him cease or be rejected. Catechumen or believers who want to become soldiers should be rejected, because they have despised God.[8]

For the early church, the general call had specific consequences for the ways converts earned a living. Some "crafts and professions" were considered appropriate for Christians; others were not. With the toleration of Christianity under Constantine, and later the recognition of Christianity as the official religion of the Roman Empire, the list of approved professions changed decisively. For instance, service as a magistrate or soldier was no longer prohibited when the Empire was considered Christian. Still, all Christians were considered called to the life of faith and service. The specifics of what forms of earning one's living could and could not be allowed as consistent with the call of God changed depending on the social context.

Another consequence of Christianity's adoption as the official religion of the empire was the rise of monasticism. With the end of persecution, many Christians felt called by God to demonstrate their faith in a manner that would set them apart from the "ordinary" Christian. One of the more popular ways of doing so in the fourth and fifth centuries was for devout men and women to renounce family and goods for a life of perpetual prayer. This monastic movement in the church led to a limiting of the idea of vocation (calling) to those who entered these intentional communities of men and women devoted to the life of prayer. By the time of the sixteenth century Reformation, Christians were commonly divided into "the religious" (those who followed the monastic way, who had a call to a religious vocation) and "secular" Christians. Secular Christians could participate in and benefit from the devotion of the religious by endowing monasteries. But secular

---

[8] Hippolytus, *The Apostolic Tradition*, trans. Geoffrey J. Cuming, as quoted in James F. White, *Documents of Christian Worship* (Louisville: Westminster/John Knox Press, 1992), p. 151-52.

Christians (and even "secular" priests) were often considered inferior to the "religious" Christians who truly lived out their faith.

Vocation in Luther and Calvin

At the time of the Protestant Reformation in the sixteenth century, Martin Luther rejected the restriction of the idea of vocation or calling to monastic life. Such division of Christians into "secular" and "religious" Luther found flawed on several counts. First, he had found from personal experience that the life of monastic rigor could not bring him to peace with God. The attempt to earn God's favor through renunciation of the world Luther found to be seriously at odds with the doctrine of God's free grace in Jesus Christ.

Instead, Luther committed himself to a recovery of the idea of the "priesthood of believers." The general call to discipleship was elevated to a place of priority over the specific calling of God. What distinguishes ordained ministers from other disciples, according to Luther, is not that they are called, and lay Christians are not. Ordained ministers, as a part of their calling, are set apart for a specific function within the life of the community. The distinction is not hierarchical. Nor is it a distinction of piety, as if clergy are more religious than lay Christians. The distinction is one of function. God's gift of leadership in the church is "to equip the saints for the work of ministry" (Eph. 4:11-13). All Christians are ministers of the gospel. Within that one ministry, we have a variety of gifts for many different types of service.

While calling into question the two-tiered piety of medieval Catholicism and the clericalism of the church, Luther did not completely do away with the distinction between clergy and laity, as some of the more radical reformers did. In this, Calvin and the Reformed tradition followed Luther. Ordination to a specialized ministry of preaching and administering sacraments was retained by Lutherans and the Reformed. But that ordination was seen as a functional distinction given by God for the purpose of serving the general calling to ministry of all disciples of Jesus Christ.

In developing his idea of vocation, Luther urged all Christians to see themselves as called, not only to be disciples of Jesus Christ, but to their particular station in life. Farmers, merchants, and nurses were encouraged to see their work as a part of their calling to serve God. The "lowest" domestic servant had a God-given purpose every bit as important as that of the pastor or teacher or magistrate. A Christian's calling includes doing his or her duty, in family, society, and church, as a sacred calling.[9]

Luther's concept of vocation was revolutionary in its day. It gave new value to work, challenging the medieval division of the world into sacred and secular. All work could be done as religious work, if done in God's service and for the sake of loving one's neighbor. But Luther's idea of vocation was also deeply conservative in many senses. One should not question one's given place in society, but see it as a part of God's purpose. There was no sense that a person should seek God's purpose apart from one's given station in life. The cobbler's son should be content in the knowledge that by his birth, God had called him to continue his father's work, even if that work was infused with new religious vitality.

At this point, Calvin's doctrine of vocation presented an advance beyond Luther. Calvin did not believe that one should simply accept one's given station in life. A Christian must actively seek his or her calling. Calvin agreed with Luther that God calls persons to many different occupations, but he refused to limit the concept of vocation to the occupation dictated by one's birth. God's calling may lead some Christians to change occupations or professions. "It would be asking far too much," Calvin wrote, "if a tailor were not permitted to learn another trade, or a merchant to change to farming."[10] A person may feel called by God to different occupations at different times in her life. Thus the Reformed

---

[9] See Gustaf Wingren, *Luther on Vocation* (Philadelphia: Muhlenberg Press, 1957).
[10] John Calvin, *The First Epistle of Paul the Apostle to the Corinthians*, Calvin's New Testament Commentaries, ed. David W. and Thomas F. Torrance, trans. John W. Fraser (Grand Rapids: Eerdmans, 1960), p. 153. Quoted in Donald K. McKim, "The 'Call' in the Reformed Tradition," in *Major Themes in the Reformed Tradition*, ed. McKim (Grand Rapids: Eerdmans, 1992), p. 340.

tradition, while agreeing with Luther's emphasis on the vocation of all Christians, developed a more dynamic approach to discerning the call of God on one's life.[11]

Recovering Vocation

The Puritans who settled New England carried the Reformed tradition's emphasis on vocation with them across the Atlantic. The Puritan work ethic has been the subject of much debate, but whatever its limitations or corruptions, it certainly led Puritan Christians to understand their work, in whatever form, as a part of their religious calling. John Wesley, who had been deeply influenced by English Puritanism, counseled his followers to "Earn all you can; save all you can; give all you can." Thus every form of earning a living could be turned to the service of God's purpose in the world.

In our time, when the concept of vocation has been divorced from its Christian roots and secularized, many Reformed Christians are arguing for a renewal of the concept of vocation. The word "vocation" has come in popular usage to be a synonym for "profession" or "job." There is little sense among many Christians of any connection between the work they do to make a living and their calling to be disciples of Jesus Christ. Work and faith are too often compartmentalized into different and unrelated arenas of life. Ironically, among Protestants today the idea is prevalent that ordained clergy are the ones who have been called; other Christians work "secular jobs" to support the "religious" work of clergy and missionaries. The medieval division of work into secular and sacred has reappeared as strong as ever.

As Wendell Berry notes, preachers are the ones we speak of as being in "full-time Christian service." In his experience, Berry notes that this term is used

> exclusively to refer to the ministry, thereby at once making of
> the devoted life a religious specialty or career and removing the

---

[11] See also John H. Leith, *John Calvin's Doctrine of the Christian Life* (Louisville: Westminster/ John Knox Press, 1989); and Ronald S. Wallace, *Calvin's Doctrine of the Christian Life* (Edinburgh: Oliver & Boyd, 1959).

possibility of devotion from other callings. Thus the $50,000-a-year preacher is a "full-time Christian servant," whereas a $20,000- or a $10,000-a-year farmer, or a farmer going broke, so far as the religious specialists are concerned must serve "the economy" in his work or in his failure and serve God in his spare time. The professional class is likewise free to serve itself in its work and to serve God by giving the church its ten percent.[12]

For Berry, the consequence of our modern clericalism is not only the separation it creates between clergy and laity, but more importantly the loss of a sense of calling about our work, whether we farm or engage in professional work or any other type of employment. The economy, business, and professional work are seen as realms outside our Christian faith and commitment, rather than areas in which we are to live out our calling as disciples of Jesus Christ.

Not all Christians have a deep internal sense of call about their employment. But some do have as strong a sense of God's having called them to teach children or practice medicine or farm or any number of different means of working as any ordained minister. Though it may sometimes be the case that what distinguishes the call to service experienced by clergy and laity is the intensity of the sense of call, this is certainly not always true. Those Christians who feel deeply a call to some other ministry besides that of ordination to pastoral ministry should know that their call is honored by the church, not discounted as in any way less important that a call to ordained ministry of word and sacrament. Those whose employment is not undertaken out of a strong sense of God's call, should be encouraged to find creative ways to live out their general calling as Christians within the context of their work.

---

[12] Wendell Berry, from *What Are People For?* (New York: North Point Press, 1990), as quoted in *From Christ to the World: Introductory Readings in Christian Ethics*, ed. Wayne G. Boulton, Thomas D. Kennedy, and Allen Verhey (Grand Rapids: Eerdmans, 1996), p. 525.

Particular Callings within the life of the Covenant Community

In the epistles of the New Testament, there is a clear understanding that God calls members of the community of faith to particular tasks within the church. These particular callings are closely related to what Paul identifies as spiritual gifts. Within the household of faith there is a great diversity of gifts given so that together, the church may grow in grace and faith. "The gifts Christ gave are that some should be apostles, some prophets, some evangelists, some pastors and teachers, to equip the saints for the work of ministry, for building up the body of Christ . . ." (Eph. 4:11-12; see also 1 Corinthians 12:1-31; Romans 12:3-8). Every gift is given for the sake of building up the church for its ministry in the world.

In recent years, many churches have conducted workshops and conferences on spiritual gifts, in which members are encouraged to identify their own gifts for the work of ministry. Once the gifts are identified, members are encouraged to find ways to exercise those gifts within the life of their particular congregation and its ministry. Such spiritual gifts workshops are one example of an attempt to recover a focus on the particular call of God to every Christian within the general call to faith and service. Theologically, this is an emphasis that lies at the heart of our own tradition as Reformed Christians.

Those who are gifted by the Spirit for teaching should be encouraged to put their gift to work for the church and its ministry. Those who have the gift of hospitality need to be identified and enlisted in the church's work of welcoming strangers into the life of the church. Some members have the ability to oversee the property of the church, and others have gifts for planning, or generosity, or ministries with the poor or homeless, or caring for the sick and dying. The list could go on and on. Within the one call of God to faith and service, there are also particular callings to specific tasks within the household of faith. It is the church's task to assist all its people to discern their particular calling and how it can serve God's larger purpose in the world.

Within the Reformed tradition there has been special emphasis on God's call to three particular offices within the church: that of deacon, elder, and Minister of Word and Sacrament. Those who enter one of these offices are called by God, through the voice of the church, to exercise leadership within the community of faith for the sake of the ministry of the whole church. While there is much greater attention given to the call to the ministry of word and sacrament, the church should emphasize that every call to one of these offices should be seen as a call from God. The first question to prospective elders and deacons should be, "You have been called by the church to lead us in our ministry. Do you feel yourself called by God to this office in the church?"

Some particular churches have found that the most effective way to recruit members for various tasks within the life of the church is to do so by issuing a "call." Instead of asking for volunteers, committees responsible for securing teachers for the church school, for instance, consider who in the church has the gifts necessary to do the work. Then those persons are issued a "call" to serve. Those issuing the call are prepared to say why they think the person's gifts and talents are suited to the particular task. The person is free to accept or reject the call, of course, but such a call often prompts persons to serious reflection about whether or not God is truly calling them to this ministry within the church. Such a "call system" is fully consistent with our theological commitment as Cumberland Presbyterians to the idea that all Christians have particular gifts and callings within the community of faith.

The Particular Call to the Ministry of Word and Sacrament

Over forty years ago, H. Richard Niebuhr proposed that the call to ordained ministry of word and sacrament includes in addition to the general call to discipleship at least three elements:

> [1] *the secret call*, namely, that inner persuasion or experience whereby a person feels himself [or herself] directly summoned or invited by God to take up the work of the [ordained] ministry; [2] *the providential call*, which is that invitation and command to assume the work of the [ordained] ministry which

comes through the equipment of a person with the talents necessary for the exercise of the office and through the divine guidance of his [or her] life by all its circumstances; [3] *the ecclesiastical call*, that is, the summons and invitation extended to a [person] by some community or institution of the Church to engage in the work of the ministry [of word and sacrament].[13]

What Niebuhr said about the call to ordained ministry of word and sacrament could easily be said of the call for all Christians. In other words, all Christians should work to discern their secret call. Each should be challenged to assess their gifts and the circumstances of life for what they may contribute to their understanding of God's call. Finally, every Christian should listen to the voice of the church and its invitation to specific ministries of service. Thus, all of what will be said about call in this section can be applies to the particular call of all Christians. But for now, we turn our attention to the call to ordained ministry of word and sacrament.

At various times in history, more or less emphasis has been given to one or another of Niebuhr's three elements of the call to ordained ministry of word and sacrament. In the early church, there was relatively little emphasis on the internal call. For instance, Augustine, Bishop of Hippo, intended after his conversion to Christianity to spend his life in a lay monastic community, in a life of study and writing. However, while he was attending a service in the nearby city of Hippo, on the North African coast, the local bishop and people recognized him. He had already made something of a name for himself through his writings in defense of the Christian faith. On the spot, the people of Hippo called Augustine to be a priest in their city, refusing his protests, unwilling to take "no" for an answer. As Augustine later recounted, "I came to this city to see a friend, whom I thought I might gain for God, that he might live with us in the monastery. I felt secure, for the place already had a bishop. I was grabbed. I was made a priest . . . and from there, I became your bishop."[14] Against his own wishes,

---

[13] H. Richard Niebuhr, The Purpose of the Church and Its Ministry (New York: Harper & Row, 1956), p. 64.

Augustine agreed to accept the people's call as the call of God on his life, and he settled in Hippo for the duration of his long and distinguished career, devoting himself to the task of serving as priest, then assistant bishop, and finally as bishop. Had he followed his own desires, Augustine would have preferred the secluded life of a scholar, but the ecclesiastical call overpowered his own sense of God's call in his life.

Similarly, John Calvin, the great sixteenth century Reformer of Geneva, did not set out to be a public leader of the Reform movement in Switzerland. He detoured through Geneva on his way to Strasbourg because the more direct route from his native city was blocked by war. In Strasbourg, he intended to take up a life similar to what Augustine had envisioned for himself. Calvin thought his gifts could best be used as a scholar and writer for the Reformed cause. But upon hearing that Calvin was in Geneva, the fiery leader of the Reform in Geneva, William Farel, went to the inn where Calvin was staying and urged him to settle in the city. When Calvin refused, Farel threatened him with the wrath of God. "You are simply following your own desires. And I tell you in the name of Almighty God, that if you refuse to take part in the Lord's work in this church, God will curse the quiet life that you want for your studies."[15] Calvin, unable to convince himself that it was *not* God's will that he stay, agreed to help Farel with the reform of the Genevan Church. With the exception of a three-year exile in Strasbourg, Calvin would spend the rest of his life as a pastor and leader of the Genevan Church. For Calvin, as for Augustine, the ecclesiastical call preceded any sense of internal call to ordained ministry.

---

[14] Augustine, Sermon 355, 2, as quoted in Peter Brown, *Augustine of Hippo* (Berkeley: University of California Press, 1967), p. 138. The full account of Augustine's call to be priest and bishop in Hippo is recounted in Brown, pp. 138-145.

[15] This incident is recounted in Dawn DeVries, "'The Meaning of Call and Ordination' A Theological Perspective," http://www.utsva.edu/copy/newspubs/Publications/focus-devries_themeaning.html.

By contrast, most Protestant churches in the United States, at least since the Great Awakening of the 1740s, have placed a much larger emphasis on what Niebuhr calls the "secret call," or , as it is more commonly designated in the Cumberland Presbyterian tradition, the "internal call." Gilbert Tennent's 1741 sermon, "The Danger of an Unconverted Ministry," was one of the more incendiary tracts of the Awakening period. In it, Tennent accused the majority of Presbyterian ministers not only of *not* having an internal call to ordained ministry, but of being bereft any true piety. For leaders of the Awakening, it was essential that one be able to narrate one's experience of conversion and call. The Cumberland Presbyterian Church, as a product of what has been called the second Great Awakening, clearly stands in this tradition of elevating the importance of the internal call.

As Joe Ben Irby notes, the *Westminster Confession* makes no reference to the internal call. But the *Constitution* of the Cumberland Presbyterian Church has since 1814 instructed its presbyteries to test the "real piety" of candidates for ordained ministry and "to examine them respecting their experimental acquaintance with religion, and the motives which influence them to desire the sacred office. *And their internal call to this important work.*"[16] Irby concludes that "Cumberland Presbyterians have from the beginning emphasized the necessity and importance of an 'internal call' to the ministry. Such a call takes precedence over an 'ecclesiastical call' . . ."[17]

Both the *Confession of 1883* and the *Confession of 1984* continue the emphasis on the internal call.[18] However, the *Confession of 1984* seems to move away from Irby's contention that the internal call takes precedence over the ecclesiastical in the provision that a "licentiate shall be ordained only if he or she has a call to a church or to a ministry approved by the presbytery."[19] While this

---

[16] *Confession of 1814*, Form of Government XII, 2; as quoted in Irby, *This They Believed: A Brief History of Doctrine in the Cumberland Presbyterian Church* (Chelsea, MI: Joe Ben Irby, 1997), p. 546. Italics added by Irby.
[17] Irby, p. 546.
[18] References to the internal call can also be found in the *1883 Constitution*, paragraphs 51 and 56; and in the *1984 Constitution*, sections 6.14, 6.15, 6.32, and 6.36.

constitutional provision has long been a part of the practice of other Presbyterian bodies, it was new to Cumberland Presbyterian practice with the *Confession of 1984*. It represents a renewed insistence that the ecclesiastical call be taken into consideration before a licentiate is ordained to the ministry of word and sacrament.[20]

Still, Irby's contention that the internal call takes priority over all other aspects of the call probably continues to reflect the practice of many Cumberland Presbyterians and the presbyteries' committees on ministry. Where that is the case, committees find it difficult to question a candidate's call, and to help the candidate examine his or her call, to test whether he or she has heard God's call rightly. A common attitude seems to be, "If a person claims to be called to the ministry of word and sacrament, who are we to question that call?" Ultimately, such an attitude on the part of committees does no service to those who, sincerely believing themselves to be called, do not exhibit the gifts and graces necessary to the fulfilling of the office of ordained minister of word and sacrament in the church. Such persons, sometimes after years of preparation for ordained ministry, may find themselves unable to secure a call to exercise their ministry. They may rightly wonder why no church will call them as pastor. They have, after all, satisfied their committee on ministry. When a committee finds itself unable to question seriously a person's providential call, that is, a person's abilities to do the work of ordained ministry, it can unwittingly set up a candidate for a lifetime of frustration. The providential call and the ecclesiastical call need to be considered as important to the long term viability of church leaders as the internal call.

---

[19] Constitution 1984, 6.31, p. 48.

[20] Recent Cumberland Presbyterian authors who have emphasized the ecclesiastical call include Morris Pepper, *An Introduction to Christian Ministry for Lay and Clergy Persons in the Cumberland Presbyterian Church*, ed. Mark Brown and James Knight (1992), pp. 21-22; and John Ed Gardner, "The Biblical Basis of Call," unpublished paper presented at the Cumberland Presbyterian Christian Education Conference (date unavailable).

That does not mean that the internal call is unimportant. It is essential if a person is to have the spiritual resources for the demanding work of pastoral leadership. But the Cumberland Presbyterian Church has always affirmed that zeal alone, without education, and without gifts for leadership, will not serve effectively the larger ministry of the people of God. The ideal call is one in which the internal sense of call, the gifts for ministry given by the Spirit, and the church's confirmation of the call come together to empower ordained ministers for the work of leading the covenant community in its response to God's call to discipleship.

Our near exclusive focus on the internal call can also lead the church to take a passive approach to identifying potential leaders for the church. Unlike the church of Augustine's and Calvin's time, we often wait patiently for persons to hear the internal voice of God, rather than identifying those with gifts for leadership in the church and challenging them to discern whether or not they should interpret those gifts and graces, and the church's need of their leadership, as a part of God's providential and ecclesiastical call on their life. Again, this is not to say that the internal call is unimportant; only that a person's serious consideration of the internal call may at times be prompted by the external call and challenge of the church.

The variety of experience among those who hear and respond to God's particular call to ordained leadership in the church is such that no one pattern can cover all cases. Morris Pepper has identified nine different means through with God may call persons.

The call may come through:

1. *The life and fellowship of the church and the influence of the gospel in our lives.* In other words, it arises out of our own Christian experience which kindles an interest and a desire to do more.

2. *The suggestions of well meaning people.* They may ask at some time and place, "Have you ever considered the ministry?" Thus the idea is dropped into our minds. They may have

observed something about us which indicated that we had the ability to become a minister.

3. *The spiritual atmosphere* of the congregation, a conference, a church camp, or some other group may have moved us and brought the call into focus.

4. *God may speak to us through a time of worship* and/or a sermon in which the idea was born in our minds or the impression made upon us.

5. *The influence of ministers.* We may see something in them which appeals to us and makes us want to be like them. They become good models. They may be pastors or parents whose children follow in their footsteps.

6. *A direct confrontation by some person:* "Have you ever considered the ministry? Can you say you have not been called?" In the early years of our denomination such recruitment was done more than it is today.

7. *A recognition on our part* of having some ability for ministry.

8. *A challenge of need and opportunity.* Upon hearing about or observing the need for ministers, we may be challenged to consider it.

9. Or, through other means, such as *a growing conviction* over a period of time that the ministry is God's will for us. Interviews with a number of people in recent years indicate that this is the kind of experience many have had.[21]

Whatever the internal experience, God is the one who calls, and the church must test and validate that call.

Discerning the Call of God

It is seldom an easy task to discern God's particular call on our lives. One recent writer has noted that God's call comes to us in the place where our deep joys and longings meet the world's great

---

[21] Morris Pepper, *An Introduction to Christian Ministry for Lay and Clergy Persons in the Cumberland Presbyterian Church*, ed. Mark Brown and James Knight (1992), p. 21.

need. For some, finding that place is like stumbling across a pearl of great value, with little or no effort. For others, a clear call from God is more elusive. There is always something of a mystery to the call of God. Still, there are guideposts to help us in the work of discernment.

First, discovering God's call is a task of spiritual discernment. It requires prayer, study, and deep self awareness. We must constantly ask whether we are hearing God's call or our own desires. This task of discernment is not one to be undertaken alone. It requires the support and counsel of our brothers and sisters in the community of faith. Selfish motives can cloud our judgment. Trusted guides are needed to help us listen attentively for God's direction. The work of Committees on Ministry is best seen as one of spiritual direction for those who are testing their sense of call to the ordained ministry of word and sacrament.

Second, it must always be remembered that the particular call to such a ministry is God's call for the sake of the church. Ordained ministry exists for the church; the church does not exist for its ordained ministers. The particular call, if it is authentic, always serves the general call of God to the life of faith and service. Some speak of the call to ordained ministry of word and sacrament as the "highest calling in the church." However, it is easy for such an idea to lead to the kind of hierarchy of callings the Reformed tradition at its best has always resisted. There may be no higher calling in the church, but this is not the same as calling ordained ministry the highest calling. Among Christians, there is no place for speaking of "higher" or "lower;" all are in Christ Jesus. The *1984 Constitution* rejects "grades of office" in the church in its description of this ministry:

> The office of minister of word and sacrament is unique in the life of the church as to responsibility and usefulness. God calls persons and sets them apart for this ministry. The persons who fill this office should be sound in the faith, exemplary in conduct, and competent to perform the duties of the ministry. Persons who become ministers of the word and sacrament are due such respect as belongs to their office, but are not by virtue

of their office more holy or righteous than other Christians. They share in the same vocation that belongs to all Christians to be witnesses to the gospel in word and deed. They differ from other Christians only with regard to the office to which they are called, which is their station in life. (1984 *Constitution*, section 2.61)

The distinction is one of responsibility, not of status. Those who seek leadership in the church out of a desire for status or prestige have not heard the call of God rightly. The call to ordained ministry is a call to live as a servant of the servants of God.

Often, those who present themselves to the church as candidates for ordained ministry have different levels of certainty about their call. This is to be expected. The probationary period is a time for testing the call. As educational and spiritual preparation for ordained ministry progresses, persons will often have their sense of call confirmed. Of course, others may decide that their original sense of call was mistaken.

The experience of Louisa Woosley, the first woman ordained to the ministry of word and sacrament in the Cumberland Presbyterian Church provides an interesting study of how one person's call was confirmed through her study and practice of ministry. Woosley recounts an internal call to ministry that she experienced soon after her conversion. But she knew of no women ministers in her time, so over time she decided that she must be mistaken about her sense of call. As a young woman, she resolved to get her husband to respond on her behalf, but he resisted. She resolved to study the Bible from beginning to end, hoping to find there an answer to her questions. At the end of almost a year of study, she became convinced that the scriptures did not prohibit women preachers. Still, she hesitated, knowing she would encounter opposition in the church. She literally became sick with her struggle, and finally resolved to respond to God's call. Again, something held her back, but when her daughter was stricken with an illness and expected to die, she promised God that she would preach if God would spare her daughter. The daughter recovered, and Woosley knew what she had to do. Still, she did not tell anyone of her sense of call, resolving to wait for an opportunity to speak in public.

Soon the session of her church called on her to lead the evening service when the pastor was absent. In the experience of standing before the church, she felt the first confirmation of her call, despite the opposition of many of her friends and family members. Later that year she presented herself for candidacy in Nolin Presbytery, and was ordained in November 1889. At first, she rarely was called to preach, but soon her services as an evangelist and preacher were in great demand. In that, again, she found confirmation of God's call, despite the fact that the General Assembly refused to seat her and instructed her presbytery to drop her name from the roll of ordained ministers.[22]

Louisa Woosley's call had all three of Niebuhr's elements. She had a strong and persistent internal call. By God's providence, she was called upon to speak at her home church, and she obviously demonstrated gifts for leadership such that her own presbytery was willing to break the unwritten tradition that women could not be ordained to the ministry of word and sacrament. Finally, the churches of her home area called her to serve them as an evangelist, providing the ecclesiastical call without which she could not have served.

The church should be willing to help those who do not find their sense of call confirmed to find their call in some other ministry of the church. Jesus' saying about "those who, having put their hand to the plow, turn back" is not directed to ministers of the word and sacrament. It is directed to those who turn back from the call to discipleship.

It is to them that Jesus directs the warning about not being fit for God's kingdom. A minister of the word and sacrament who feels called to give up his or her office in the church should not be shamed. On the other hand, the church must always take care to

---

[22] Louisa Woosley's eloquent account of her call is recounted in the last chapter of her book, Shall Woman Preach, Or the Question Answered (Canneyvill, KY, 1891); reprinted by the Cumberland Presbyterian Board of Christian Education (Memphis: Frontier Press, 1989), pp. 96-101.

see that those who have responded to this particular call are encouraged and supported in their ministry as long as that ministry promises useful for the life of the church.

The Call to Particular Persons as Pastors

Any discussion of the call would be incomplete without a brief discussion of our call system for matching ordained ministers with particular churches. Churches with Presbyterian government have long cherished the call system. Churches, through their sessions, call whom they will to serve as their pastor. Pastors are free to accept or decline calls from particular churches. At its best, our system values the desires and needs of both pastors and people, rather than depending on a system of appointment for assigning pastoral leadership to churches.

One of the liabilities of the call system, however, is that if often fails to serve the needs of both pastors and churches. Rural churches often find it difficult to attract candidates for pastor. Many pastors, especially women and older men, find it difficult to get churches to consider them for a call. What many have spoken of recently as a "crisis in pastoral leadership" in our church is not due to a lack of ordained pastors. We have many pastors who are under-employed because they do not fit the profile of what churches are looking for in their "ideal" pastor. While there are no easy answers to the difficulty we are experiencing in this matter, churches and pastors should be challenged to examine whether their idea of call is grounded in God's will. The task of spiritual discernment in this area of the call is as critical as in any other.

Some churches need to be educated to understand the difference between calling a pastor and hiring a chief executive officer. The call to a person to be pastor of a particular congregation must be undertaken in the spirit of God's general call to the church to be a faithful witness to the gospel of Jesus Christ. At the same time, pastors should have a clear sense of the difference between entertaining a call and climbing a career ladder.

God's call to us as Cumberland Presbyterians in the 21st century demands that we look and pray for the leaders God is calling us to recognize. Sometimes those leaders will not be the ones we had previously envisioned. Like David's father Jesse, we should be prepared that we may often be surprised at who God calls. May God help us to look beyond the appearances, to the heart, both our own, and that of the leaders God graciously continues to send us, and calls us to recognize, equip, and support in our service of the one call of God in Jesus Christ.

5. Theological And Biblical Reflection On Women In Ministry

A study paper prepared by the Unified Committee on Theology and Social Concerns of the Cumberland Presbyterian Churches
Adopted for study and commended to the churches and presbyteries of the CPC by the 171st General Assembly
June 2001, Odessa, Texas

Introduction

The following study paper was prepared by Rev. Renee Curtiss, a member of the Unified Committee on Theology and Social Concerns of the Cumberland Presbyterian Churches, at the request of the Committee. In planning its agenda, the Committee had decided that we needed to provide this biblical and theological resource for the Cumberland Presbyterian Churches to assist their members in understanding the two churches' position of support for ordaining women to the work of the gospel ministry. The paper was edited by the Unified Committee, and forwarded to the General Assemblies of the CPC and CPCA meeting in June of 2001.

The 171st meeting of the CPC General Assembly approved this study paper for use throughout the church. In so doing, the Assembly passed the following recommendation:

That presbyterial Boards of Missions and local congregations be strongly encouraged to study this issue [women in ministry] in light of the Cumberland Presbyterian Church's stated position of gender equality and with the intention of encouraging changed attitudes among those who do not see fit to consider female pastoral leadership. The Unified Committee's theological reflection is to be one resource, among many possible resources, for this study.

The GA committee that studied this issue went on to state "that building relationships between women in ministry and congregations is the key to change regarding this issue. We ... suggest that interim pastors help in this education and relationship-building process. In addition, where possible, presbyterial Boards of Missions are encouraged to appoint female moderators of sessions. Regardless of gender, the appointed moderator should help in the education process and encourage the church to consider female applicants for pastors and staff positions; and finally, to encourage congregations to consider inviting women in ministry to fill the pulpit for revivals, vacations, times of illness, and special occasions."

We send out this study paper with the prayer that the Holy Spirit will continue to help us as a church welcome the gifts and ministries of those whom God has called to the gospel ministry, women and men alike.

Theological and Biblical Reflection on Women in Ministry

A Study paper prepared for the Unified Committee on Theology and Social Concerns, February 23, 2001 by Renee A. Curtiss

Although the Cumberland Presbyterian Church has been ordaining women to the office of Word and Sacrament since 1889, the practice is still one that is disputed and hotly debated at the grass roots level. The 1984 Constitution and Confession of Faith, clearly support the ordination of women to the offices of pastor, elder and deacon. As a denomination, we are proud to have been the first Presbyterian body to ordain a woman. The ordination of Louisa M. Woosley in 1889 was however, marked by an enormous theological debate within the denomination.

Our internal statistics, as well as the personal experiences of most clergywomen, indicate that the issue is far from settled, even in the year 2001. For this reason, the Unified Committee on Theology and Social Concerns, offers this paper as a resource for studying and evaluating the issue of women in ministry and leadership within the Cumberland Presbyterian Church.

As with any topic within the church, it is absolutely essential that a thorough and sound theological and biblical foundation be the bedrock upon which all praxis is derived. Therefore we will begin our study here.

It seems appropriate and logical then, to begin at the beginning. Genesis 1:26 (NRSV):

> *Then God said, 'Let us make humankind*
> *(Hebrew: Adam)*
> *in our image according to our likeness; and let them*
> *have dominion over the fish of the sea, and over the*
> *birds of the air, and over the cattle, and over all the*
> *wild animals of the earth and over every creeping*
> *thing that creeps upon the earth.' So God created*
> *humankind in God's image, in the image of God,*
> *God created them, male and female God created them.*
> *[. . . . .]*
> *God saw everything that God had made and indeed, it was very good.*

This creation story is the first of two and is often overlooked or even forgotten in light of the Adam and Eve story. Let us take a closer look at these two creation accounts. It will be helpful to note the Hebrew at some points which will be bracketed and italicized. Genesis 1:27 says:

> *So God created humankind [adam: human being,*
> *no sexual connotation] in God's image, in the image*
> *of God he created them; male [zakar] and female*
> *[neqebah] he created them;*

or in another rendering: "male and female created he them and called their name 'Adam'" – humankind." Human nature, not masculinity, is "in the image of God," and this human nature consists of maleness and femaleness. There is no suggestion of inferiority or superiority of any kind.

Another perspective of the image here is reflected on by Grenz, who says that ultimately what it·means to reflect God's image is to be in relationship or community. Our God is a God of community as any doctrine of the Trinity will clearly indicate. Throughout all eternity, God is community, the fellowship of the Three Persons who constitute the triune God. Grenz states:

> *As the first creation narrative declares, when God created humankind, God built into creatures – created male and female – the unity-in-diversity and mutuality that characterize the eternal divine reality. Consequently, neither the male as such nor the isolated human is the image of God. Instead humans-in-relation or humans in community ultimately reflect the imago Dei. Such human fellowship encompasses diversity and illustrates mutuality (p.171).*

So we deduce, God establishes a covenant relationship with all of humanity, not just the male portion.

Let us now turn our concentration to the second creation account, which has historically been interpreted by many in such a way as to justify the subjugation and subordination of women to men and therefore used as a basis for denying women the ability to serve in leadership positions within the church.

The second chapter of Genesis records: "In the day that the Lord God made the earth and the heavens, then the Lord God formed man [adam] from the dust of the ground." When creation of the physical world – plants and animals – is completed, there is still something to be desired "but for the man there was not found a helper as his partner" (Gen. 2:20b), one who will be with him. The term "help" or "helper," [ezer] is found twenty-one times in the Old Testament, twice in this chapter. From the other nineteen uses, sixteen times the help is God; the other three speak of relative equals. Never does the word connote subordination. When the text speaks of God as our help [ezer], it is of course acknowledging God's strength and power for us, not God's subordination to us. Isn't it ironic then, that we would want to interpret [ezer] in the context of Genesis 2 as meaning subordinate? When God creates Eve from Adam's rib, God's intent is that she will be – unlike the animals – a power (or strength) equal to him.

The second term "meet" (KJV), "fit" (RSV), or "partner" (NRSV) is a translation of [neged], a preposition. Elsewhere in the Old Testament it is translated as "before," "in the presence of," "in the sight of," "over against." The sense in this verse has been rendered as "a mirror image of himself, in which he recognized himself." We may conclude that neither term [ezer or neged] indicates subordination of one to the other. According to Grenz:

> *The creation of woman 'for man' or as his 'helper' means that*
> *she rescues him from his solitude — 'then God said it is not*
> *good that the man should be alone' (Gen.2:18) Rather than*
> *being cast in a subservient role, she is thereby elevated in the*
> *narrative as the crowning achievement of God's saving intent*
> *in the Garden (p. 165).*

It is important to note here, that our interpretation of a text depends on where we are standing. We cannot deny the presuppositions that we bring to a text and how they impact our interpretation. It is however, our responsibility to be aware of these biases in our reflection.

To those who still insist that the woman being taken out of the man's rib, is subordinate, the first ruler, the second ruled, we might recall that "the Lord God formed man from the dust of the ground"(Gen.2:7a). The words contain a point not reproducible in English: for, in the Hebrew, 'ground' [adamah] is in form the feminine of 'man' [adam].

We see the coming into being of woman. A most profound image: God builds woman out of man's "essential stuff." There could be no clearer picture than this: the most intimate belonging to each other. Adam was incomplete without his counterpart; now human nature is complete. "Therefore a man leaves his father and his mother and clings to his wife" (Gen.2:24a). The "therefore" speaks of their oneness in completing each other.

The creation accounts in chapters one and two of Genesis depict a humanity created in the image of God. This humanity is to be in a relationship of mutuality and equality, recognizing the divine image in one another and their need for interdependence and mutual support. The Confession of Faith in section 1.11 summarizes it this way:

> *Among all forms of life, only human beings are*
> *created in God's own image. In the sight of God, male and female*
> *are created equal and complementary. To reflect the divine image*
> *is to worship, love, and serve God.*

If this is the proper order of creation, then why the need for this paper? We need not look far for the answer. Genesis 3 offers an explanation for the disruption of the original order.

Put simply, the disintegration and disruption is a result of sin and the Fall.

> *To the woman God said, 'I will greatly*
> *increase your pangs in childbearing;*
> *in pain you shall bring forth children, yet*
> *your desire shall be for your husband,*
> *and he shall rule over you.'*

This is not the way God created things to be, but because of sin, it is the way God has allowed things to be. It is precisely at this point that the relationship of mutuality between male and female was corrupted, leading instead to a relationship of discrimination and subjugation of women to men.

By the grace of God, however, this is not the final word. Christ is the Alpha and the Omega and it is he who has the last word on any and all issues. The final say is this — Christ redeems us (all humanity) from sin and is the restorer of the original order. We are no longer living under the curse of sin, but under the grace of God through the atoning sacrifice of Jesus Christ. As stated in 2 Corinthians 5:17, "So if anyone is in Christ, there is a new creation; everything old has passed away: see, everything has become new!" Also from Galatians 3:27-28: "As many of you as were baptized into Christ have clothed yourselves with Christ. There is no longer Jew or Greek, there is no longer slave or free, there is no longer male and female; for all of you are one in Christ Jesus."

God invites us to work in this new kingdom order through the power of the Holy Spirit. The Spirit chooses to work where the Spirit wishes and with whom the Spirit wishes. The spirit's freedom of movement is noted in Joel 2:28-32 and again in Acts 2 on the day of Pentecost. Acts 1:13-14 states:

> *When they had entered the city, they went to*
> *the room upstairs where they were staying,*
> *Peter, and John, and James, and Andrew, Philip*
> *and Thomas, Bartholomew and Matthew, James*
> *son of Alphaeus, and Simon the Zealot, and Judas*
> *son of James. All these were constantly*
> *devoting themselves to prayer, together with*
> *certain women including Mary the mother*
> *of Jesus, as well as his brothers.*

On Pentecost when all of these were filled with the Holy Spirit, Peter stood up and recited from the prophet Joel:

> *In the last days it will be, God declares*
> *that I will pour out my Spirit upon all flesh,*
> *and your sons and your daughters shall*
> *prophesy, and your young men shall see*
> *visions, and your old men shall dream*
> *dreams. Even upon my slaves both men*
> *and women, in those days I will pour out*
> *my Spirit; and they shall prophesy.*

Not only is there evidence in scripture that the Spirit works in many and various ways — but the evidence of this is before our very eyes. The Spirit is unbounded and works in and through persons without regard to their ethnicity, nationality, social-economic status, intellect, education, age, or yes, even gender.

It is also important to note the historical Jesus' attitude toward women. He more often than not, defied the traditions and customs of his time. He talked to women, even to the despised ones: to the woman of Samaria (John 4:17); the Syrophoenician woman (Mark 7:24) whom he commended for her faith.

He accepted women's ministry to and for him. He taught them, an unheard of thing at that time, and called them not to limit their work to "housewifely" ministrations. "Mary, who sat at the Lord's feet and listened to what he was saying" (Luke 10:39) was commended, for she understood that "there is need of only one thing" (Luke 10:42a). She had chosen "the better part which will not be taken away" (Luke 10:42b). Jesus allowed a woman who was a "sinner" to wash and anoint his feet saying: "Your sins are forgiven" (Luke 7:48b). He healed men and women; accepted a woman's precious oil to anoint him for burial and included her in the proclamation of the gospel: "wherever the good news is proclaimed in the whole world, what she has done will be told in remembrance of her" (Mark 14:9; Matthew 26:6). Women went with him on the road to Golgotha, and they were the last ones to whom he spoke before the crucifixion (Luke 23:27). They went to see where Joseph of Arimathea laid him (Mark 15:47 & parallels) and when the Sabbath had passed, they went back with the spices. At the empty tomb the women were the ones to hear the white robed figures announce: "he has been raised; go, tell his disciples and Peter" (Mark 16:6-7). The women "told this to the apostles. But these words seemed to them an idle tale, and they did not believe them" (Luke 24:10-11). It was a woman (John 20:11-18; women in Matt. 28:1-10) who was first greeted by the Risen Lord.

Initiation into this new community replaces the covenant sign of Israel that marks only the male members of the community. The right of baptism is the same to men and women who die and rise with Christ. Women thus are joint heirs and announcers of the good news.

Many commentators and Christians consider that the absence of women among the Twelve speaks against women in spiritual office. These same observers fail to note that, if this were true, it would speak against Gentiles in spiritual office too. The eleven Jews, aware that Judas's place has to be taken, consider two other Jews and cast lots for them. True, no Gentiles are among the converts yet, and women are, but the judging of the twelve tribes was not so imminent as to exclude waiting for the Gentiles. The point is this: If in the divine economy the Twelve are to represent the new "priesthood" or authentic ministry of the gospel, they fail to represent women and Gentiles alike. The barrier between Jew and Gentile was as great as between male and female, and both barriers were removed by Christ.

It is also worth noting that some writings attributed to Paul are often noted in denying women to the office of ministry and leadership within the church. To this opposition we render a simple argument of logic. It is time for honesty and consistency in the interpretive act. If one is compelled to a literal interpretation of the scripture, then it is imperative that this be pervasively consistent. For example in I Corinthians 14, if one deems appropriate the literal interpretation of "women are to keep silent in the churches" then the praxis should reflect this interpretive approach.

Therefore, there would be no female voices in choirs or congregational singing. There would be no women praying out loud. There would be no women teaching Sunday School or Vacation Bible School. There would be no women's missionary societies or fellowships, unless that is, they were silent gatherings. The silencing of the feminine voice means all of this and more. The ramifications of which would undoubtedly be devastating to the Church.

How is it then, many have interpreted this silencing to be applicable only for positions of leadership within the church? It is time to stop proof texting for our personal advantage or status. In order to be true to the text, it is also imperative that the scripture be interpreted in light of its historical and cultural context. Paul's letters and those attributed to Paul were addressed to particular people and churches within a particular context. These churches were grappling with concrete issues which the author was attempting to specifically address.

Before making a judgment on the issue of women in leadership within the church, one must look at the writings of Paul which support the concept. Paul on his missionary journeys preached to and converted men and women, and considered men and women his fellow workers. The tentmaker couple, Aquila and Priscilla (or Prisca), with whom he dined and worked at Corinth, and sailed to Ephesus, remained his friends. When Apollos came to Ephesus and spoke in the synagogue with insufficient knowledge of the faith, "Priscilla and Aquila heard him, they took him aside and explained the Way of God to him more accurately" (Acts 18:26). Later Paul writes: "Greet Prisca and Aquila, who work with me in Christ Jesus" (Rom. 16:3). The long list of greetings found in Romans 16 includes the names of eighteen men and eight women. It is here that we hear also of "our sister Phoebe, a deacon of the church at Cenchrae."

It is noteworthy to mention what the Confession of Faith states in 1.07: "In order to understand God's word spoken in and through the scriptures, persons must have the illumination of God's own Spirit. Moreover, they should study the writings of the Bible in their historical settings, compare scripture with scripture, listen to the witness of the church throughout the centuries, and share insights with others in the covenant community."

Gains have certainly been made regarding women in ministry, yet, we still have a long way to go. We still express our faith in words that exclude women; we still pay clergywomen lower salaries than we pay clergymen; we often regulate women to declining churches; and we still perpetuate myths and stereotypes that assign second-class status and roles to women.

A women in ministry research project in the Christian Church, Disciples of Christ in June of 1991 entitled Where We Stand makes this important note:

> *For many congregations the discrimination*
> *[against women] comes in the form of an assumption*
> *that men's competence can be trusted [as compared*
> *to women's competence]. For women, trust is*
> *rarely granted automatically, but must be tested*
> *and proven, and there is always a reserve of*
> *uncertainty in members of the congregation.*

Additional Ideas for Study

Have a debate! A week or two before the debate, hand out the study paper to each person. Divide the group/class into two different debate teams. Team #1 would argue for ordained women in ministry. Team #2 would argue against ordained women in ministry. On the day of the debate give each team 10-15 minutes to argue their point. Then allow each team a five (5) minute rebuttal. After the debate, invite open conversation about new insights and understandings gleaned from their study, preparation, and debate experience.

Guest Speaker! Invite a clergy woman to speak to your group/class about her experiences in that role. Have the group/class prepare for the conversation by reading the study paper and all suggested scripture passages. Encourage the group/class members to ask questions concerning her

*call

*preparation for ministry

*joys of ministry

*obstacles

*future plans

As closure, brainstorm ways in which you, as a group/class and a church, and we as a denomination, can be more open and inclusive to clergy women. Pick out one or two ways and covenant together as group/class to work toward that goal.

Works Cited[23]

[23] Fule, AureliaT. Should Women Keep Silence in the Churches? Louisville: Women Employed by the Church; 1992.

Grenz, Stanley J. and Denise Muir Kjesbo. Women in the Church: A Biblical Theology of Women in Ministry. Downers Grove: InterVarsity Press, 1995.

Melton, J. Gordon. The Churches Speak On: Women's Ordination. Detroit: Gale Research Inc., 1991.

Webb, Val. Why We're Equal: Introducing Feminist Theology. St. Louis: Chalice Press, 1999.

Woosley, Louisa M. Shall Woman Preach? Or the Question Answered. Caneyville, KY: n.p. 1891; Reprinted edition Memphis: Frontier Press, 1989.

PART THREE
Appendix

11. Questions For
Ordination Examination

This appendix includes questions that would appropriate for a licentiate's final exam before approved by the Committee on the Ministry for ordination.

The categories listed here are suggested in our *Confession of Faith* (*Constitution* 6:32). The Pastoral Development Ministry Team has provided several questions in each category. These questions are, however, only suggestions. Each presbytery's Committee on the Ministry will determine not only the questions to be presented to their licentiates, but also the manner of examination, written or oral.

PERSONAL FAITH AND GROWTH

1. Describe your faith pilgrimage in terms of your relationship to Christ and the church.

2. What is your understanding of the place of prayer in one's relationship with God?

3. Have you grown in your faith since you have been under the care of presbytery? In what ways?

CALL TO MINISTRY

4. Describe your sense of call. Has it changed since you responded to it? In what ways?

5. How do you interpret your calling in light of what Cumberland Presbyterians believe that all Christians are a "called" people? How is your calling different? How is it the same?

HOLY SCRIPTURES

6. What do you understand by the phrase: "…the inspiration of the scriptures?"

7. What do you understand by the phrase: "…the infallible rule of faith and practice?"

8. Why is it important to know the time frame and authorship of the books of the Bible?

9. What do you understand by the term "biblical criticism?"

10. In what ways do the synoptic gospels differ from each other? From the fourth gospel?

11. What is meant by the phrase "comparing scripture with scripture?" Why is it important? Or, what's wrong with proof texting, anyway?

12. Briefly describe the picture of Jesus presented in the Gospel of Mark.

13. Briefly describe the unity and diversity of the Bible.

14. Briefly comment on Christianity's indebtedness to Judaism in the following areas: understanding the nature of God, the covenant, law and grace.

15. What do Cumberland Presbyterians mean by the "authority of scripture?"

THEOLOGY

16. Describe your thoughts about Cumberland Presbyterian theology. Describe your feelings.

17. What are some of the principal elements of Cumberland Presbyterian theology?

18. Discuss some of the different "theories" of the atonement.

19. What is your definition of the following: sin, repentance, forgiveness, reconciliation, covenant, grace, faith, and works?

20. What does Cumberland Presbyterian theology say about the preservation of believers?

21. What does Cumberland Presbyterian theology say about the Holy Spirit?

22. Discuss the Cumberland Presbyterian theology of both sacraments: the Lord's Supper and baptism.

23. What is the importance of the resurrection for the Christian's life and the Christian faith?

24. Why are the following important to the development of Christian theology (selectively chosen): Augustine, Martin Luther, John Calvin, John Knox, Huldrych Zwingli and John Wesley.

CHURCH HISTORY

25. Discuss the growth of the early church as related in scripture.

26. What issues led to the Protestant Reformation?

27. Discuss the development of the Presbyterian/Reformed churches and the place of the Cumberland Presbyterian Church within the Reformed family of churches.

28. Briefly describe the social, political and religious conditions just prior to (1) the Great Awakening and (2) the Second Great Awakening.

29. Name some of the contributions of the Cumberland Presbyterian Church to Christianity, both nationally and internationally.

30. Briefly discuss the development of major theological movements in the 20th and 21st centuries.

PASTORAL CARE

31. Describe the pastor's role as "shepherd" to the congregation.

32. Why is confidentiality important in the pastoral role?

33. Discuss the pastor's role in counseling as related to advantages, limitations, referrals and balance with other pastoral responsibilities.

34. What are your personal guidelines for conduct when visiting in a hospital?

PREACHING AND WORSHIP

35. Is the sermon important? Why or why not?

36. What goes into making a sermon? What are its goals? What is the place of the Bible in preaching? What makes a sermon prophetic?

37. Describe your method of preparation and approach to sermon planning, preparation and preaching.

38. Name of the most commonly used lectionary. Do you use a lectionary? Why or why not?

39. What is your opinion of traditional worship, blended worship and contemporary worship?

40. How do you plan for worship? What resources do you use, if any?

NURTURE AND ADMINISTRATION

41. Among other roles, a minister is a teacher. Briefly describe your feelings about this role.

42. What are the attitudes and aptitudes needed to be an effective administrator of church programs and ministries?

THE CHURCH IN MISSION

43. What does the *Confession of Faith* say about the church in mission?

44. What is a "healthy" congregation? Describe some characteristics.

45. Describe the unity and diversity of the church.

46. What have your experiences been with connectional and independent congregations? Why have you chosen to do ministry in a connectional church?

THE CUMBERLAND PRESBYTERIAN CHURCH

47. What are the responsibilities of the session, as outlined in the *Constitution*?

48. What are the responsibilities of the presbytery, as outlined in the *Constitution*?

49. What are the responsibilities of the General Assembly, as outlined in the *Constitution*?

50. Discuss the accountability of ministers and probationers to the presbytery.

51. Discuss the accountability of sessions to the presbytery.

52. Discuss the *Constitution's* statements relating to congregational property.

53. What is the purpose of discipline, as defined in the *Rules of Discipline*?

Made in the USA
Charleston, SC
14 November 2013